12 Steps to Confidence

Survivor's Workbook
to Building Confidence and
Finding Inner Beauty

BEAUTY BEYOND THE MIRROR
12 STEPS TO CONFIDENCE

Copyright © 2016 by Andrea Grant

All rights reserved. No portion of this publication may be reproduced, distributed, or transmitted in any form or by any means, including photocopying, recording, or other electronic or mechanical methods, without the prior written permission of the publisher, except in the case of brief quotations embodied in critical reviews and certain other noncommercial uses permitted by copyright law.

For permission requests, write to the publisher, addressed "ATTN: Permissions" at the following:

Sh'Shares NETWORK, LLC
1601-1 N Main Street 13202
Jacksonville, FL 32206-0202
www.ShShares.com

Bulk discounts are available on quantity purchases by associations, corporations, and others for business, educational and ministry use. For details, contact the publisher at the address above.

Library of Congress Control Number: 2016962200

ISBN: 978-1-942650-70-6

Printed in the United States of America
FIRST EDITION

CONTENTS

Introduction 1
Letter To My Readers 2

Step 01. It Happened 3
Step 02. ACCEPTANCE 13
Step 03. Hold Your Head Up 45
Step 04. "Don't Stare! Ask Me My Story!" ... 50
Step 05. Look the Part 61
Step 06. BOUNCE BACK! 68
Step 07. Flashbacks 70
Step 08. Achieving Goals 72
Step 09. Are You a Victim or SURVIVOR? 75
Step 10. Let Go 80
Step 11. Be a Ladder 89
Step 12. You ARE a SURVIVOR!!! 91

Closing Letter 95
References 96

INTRODUCTION

August 14, 2001:

It was moments after the explosion...

I was standing in my neighbor's bathroom. He yelled to his daughters, "Take down all the mirrors!!!," yet there was one mirror that could not be removed: the mirror in the bathroom. It stayed on the wall.

My brother Kendell and I had been placed in the bathroom tub until fire and rescue teams arrived. The moment I jumped out, I looked directly into that mirror. The little girl I had seen earlier that morning while getting ready for school was not the same little girl whose eyes haunted me now.

My eyes were filled with fear. They were so big.

I have always had long, beautiful hair.

That day, I had worn it up in a ponytail.

By this point, my once fine ponytail was now crisp.

My skin was falling off my face. My lips were swelling.

I had been broken and I was slowly dying, both physically and mentally.

My heart raced.

Panic set in.

Hallucination had arrived.

The face that I had always known would never be seen the exact same way again... **in the mirror**.

I didn't know at that time what it would take to build back my confidence and ultimately find Beauty Beyond the Mirror.

LETTER TO MY READERS

Dear Victim,

I see you...

Unhappy and low on confidence. I see your life has been changed and you are now forced to deal with it. You've chosen to be bitter and angry.

Family and friends have missed the signs that you are depressed. They don't see that you only need one hug and just a few encouraging words to make it to tomorrow. You can't make it through one more bad day: another day of self-pity, the stares of people and the weight of life. Sometimes, you just want to end it all and never live to see tomorrow.

I know! **I've lived in the moment that you are in today.** With encouragement, faith and these **12 Steps to Confidence**, your path of sorrow will only be that: just a moment.

I will help you transition from being a victim to being a

SURVIVOR!

Join me along this path of telling your story so you can find the **Beauty Beyond the Mirror** using these **12 Steps to Confidence**.

I am excited about your future!

Your Friend,
Andrea Grant

STEP 01.   IT HAPPENED

Okay! Let's take a look at your new reality… It happened.

Your life has COMPLETELY changed!

You're hurt. You're angry. You're shocked and in disbelief!

I know *just* what you're thinking…

"This Sucks!"

Often, many questions are filling your head so quickly that you have NO space for answers…

> "Why did this happen to me out of ALL people?"
> "Lord, WHY?"
> "How will I make it?"
> "What will people think?"
> "WHO will help ME?"

Along with these questions and more, you are thinking that the person you once were has either died or been destroyed forever…

> "I've been changed FOREVER."
> "Who am I NOW???"
> "I don't know this person."
> "Look at my SCARS."

I know how it goes because I've been there. If nobody understands you, I do. I asked these same questions to myself and to God.

I have been raised to never question God and his actions, yet we're only human. How can we not ask questions when being faced with obstacles that permanently change our lives? I will even admit that I, too, was once angry with God.

I want to help you find the peace and understanding that I found.

You are not dead and you have not been destroyed.

Let's start your road to recovery TOGETHER!

LESSON

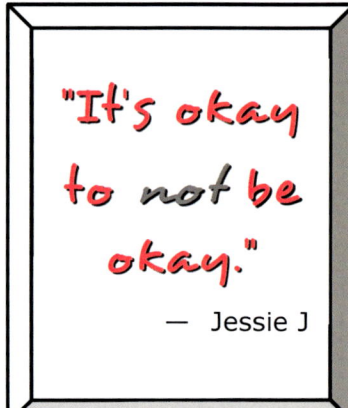

> "It's okay to not be okay."
> — Jessie J

People expect you to just live with your scars or disabilities as if it never happened. Well, guess what? You can cry! You can scream!

You don't have to be okay!

Learn to express your emotions in the best way that YOU know how. Over time, this expression will help you to heal the hurt in your heart and the confusion in your mind.

I will help you along the way!

EXERCISE

Write Your Story

Writing your story helps you to understand several things:

1. It happened.
2. There is no time machine I can get into and replay the moments to figure out "Why?"
3. I cannot take back what has happened.

My Story:

Writing my story has always been a struggle for me because I remember every detail. Whenever I write my story, I find myself reliving the scene all over again. While I write, I feel the same exact emotions I experienced during the episode that I am writing about at the time.

When telling your story—or when writing it—you may have to stop and let your mind rest. The flashbacks will be authentic *(Read More in Step 07)*. You will feel emotions that you have not felt since that day. Learn to work through those emotions. Don't avoid them. The entire process will become much easier through repetition.

Here's some help to get you started on your road to recovery.

Use the next few pages to get started with telling your story.

Share what happened…

> **What is My Story? What Happened??**

What is My Story? (Continued)

What is My Story? (Continued)

How Do I *Feel* About What Happened?

Find Someone You Trust and Read Your Story to Them.

Who Do I Trust?

Who Could I Share My Story With?

Who Should I Share My Story With?

Who Would I Share My Story With?

When Will You Share Your Story?

Using the lists that you created on the previous page, write down 20 people that you WILL share your story with. Add the date and check them off your list when you share your story.

Who WILL I Share My Story With???	DATE
1.	
2.	
3.	
4.	
5.	
6.	
7.	
8.	
9.	
10.	
11.	
12.	
13.	
14.	
15.	
16.	
17.	
18.	
19.	
20.	

How Did I Feel After Sharing My Story?

How Did Sharing Help Me Accept What Happened?

STEP 02. ACCEPTANCE

My Story:

I remember the first time my mother handed me a mirror so that I could see my face.

I had no hair.

They shaved it all off so the skin on my scalp could be placed elsewhere on my body (for skin grafts).

At the time, I did not want to accept my new image. I was bitter and angry. I was depressed.

I was YOU! I did NOT accept my new image! Why should I have to? I later learned the answer to that question...

My Friend, You Were Chosen!

"Picked out to be picked on," is the way my mother would say it to me...

...since **God knew you were *strong* enough, *tough* enough and *wise* enough** to endure the test and pass this message on to another survivor who is struggling!

LESSON

There are many lessons that come along with our path to acceptance.

- **A** Allow People to Help You
- **C** Continue to Fight
- **C** Cool Confidence in Knowing Who You Are
- **E** Express Your Feelings LOUDLY!
- **P** Persevere Through This Test
- **T** Talk! It Helps to Get Your Feelings Out!
- **A** Appreciate Your Second Chance at Life!
- **N** Never Be Ashamed of Your Past, Your Present or Your Future
- **C** Create a New Normal for Yourself
- **E** Ease into Loving Life and YOURSELF All Over Again

EXERCISE

Allow People to Help You

Family members and close friends want to help but many don't know how because when we are in pain, we're often moody, mean and sometimes very difficult to deal with.

Think about these facts and reply to the exercises below.

Who Has Tried to Help OR Connect with Me?	

In short answers, how have you responded?

My Poor Responses	My Positive Responses

How Can I Begin to Allow People to Help Me?

Once I Allow Help, What Will the Benefits Be?

What Can I Do to Create Long-Term Change?

"When the next person offers a hand, accept it."

— Andrea Grant

"When the next person offers a hand, accept it."

— Andrea Grant

Courage to Continue to Fight

We all find courage from different people and even from some places.

My Story:

When I find myself ready to give up, I find courage in my children.

Now, it's your turn! Find what brings you courage.

Where Do I Find COURAGE?		
People	Places	Things

Why is it Important to Find and Have Courage?

Why Must I Continue to Fight?

"When I find myself ready to give up, I find courage in my children."
— Andrea Grant

Write a Related Quote of Your Own—A Positive Response to Your Fight:

— (Write Your Name Here)

Confidence in Knowing Who You Are

Be confident in knowing You Are Built for This!!!

Write a few letters to encourage yourself. Fill in the blanks below to get started.

I Am:

I Can:

and I **WILL!!!**

I Have Accomplished:

I Will Accomplish:

and I Am **BUILT FOR THIS**!!!

Andrea Grant

I Am BUILT FOR THIS !!!

Express Your Feelings Loudly

Try not to whisper your feelings to yourself. Holding in how you feel will only make recovery a slow and lonely process. Let the people around you hear how you feel!

Bubble in each option that describes how you feel at this point in your life. *Add missing options in the final column.*

- ○ alone
- ○ angry
- ○ ashamed
- ○ betrayed
- ○ confused
- ○ depressed
- ○ guilty
- ○ helpless

- ○ hopeless
- ○ let down
- ○ nonchalant
- ○ pitiful
- ○ sad
- ○ selfish
- ○ tired
- ○ uncomfortable

- ○ _____
- ○ _____
- ○ _____
- ○ _____
- ○ _____
- ○ _____
- ○ _____
- ○ _____

Bubble in each option that describes how you want to feel after completing this workbook. *Add missing options in the final column.*

- ○ alive
- ○ AMAZING!
- ○ beautiful
- ○ better
- ○ bold
- ○ carefree
- ○ comforted
- ○ CONFIDENT!
- ○ courageous
- ○ ENERGIZED!
- ○ faith-filled
- ○ faithful
- ○ fearless
- ○ FOCUSED!

- ○ FREE!
- ○ friendly
- ○ good
- ○ gorgeous
- ○ GREAT!
- ○ happy
- ○ healed
- ○ healthy
- ○ hopeful
- ○ lovely
- ○ prepared
- ○ proud
- ○ READY!
- ○ whole

- ○ _____
- ○ _____
- ○ _____
- ○ _____
- ○ _____
- ○ _____
- ○ _____
- ○ _____
- ○ _____
- ○ _____
- ○ _____
- ○ _____
- ○ _____
- ○ _____

Show this page to someone you trust. Discuss both lists of feelings with them.

What Did I Learn by Discussing My Feelings?

Without saying a word, ask 3 people to share 10 words that describe your current expression.

What NEGATIVE Feelings Have I Expressed?

1.	1.	1.
2.	2.	2.
3.	3.	3.
4.	4.	4.
5.	5.	5.
6.	6.	6.
7.	7.	7.
8.	8.	8.
9.	9.	9.
10.	10.	10.

Tell those same 3 people that you are completing this workbook. Tell them you will have NEW, **confident** feelings when done. Ask them to share 10 feelings that they want you to experience after completing this workbook.

What NEW Feelings Do You Want Me to Experience?

1.	1.	1.
2.	2.	2.
3.	3.	3.
4.	4.	4.
5.	5.	5.
6.	6.	6.
7.	7.	7.
8.	8.	8.
9.	9.	9.
10.	10.	10.

What Did the Others Say About My Feelings?

Persevere Through This!
Prayer Changes Things

Follow your faith!!! Praying and crying out to God is my **1st STEP** when facing any troubling situation or burden in my life.

STOP! Take the time RIGHT NOW to say a prayer to God about your story. Make sure God knows EXACTLY how you feel. Share the GOOD, the BAD... **and the UGLY**! God understands and God cares, so share. **Stop now and PRAY!**

— Andrea Grant

... I'LL WAIT ...

After you pray OR if you can't find the words to say to God verbally, there's a mirror on the next page for you to reflect. Write your letter to God in the form of a prayer. When you're done, say the prayer out loud. Repeat your prayer to God as many times as you need to. With practice, you will become more comfortable with praying to God. Prayer will get you through the tough times, AND of course...

PRAYER CHANGES THINGS!

Andrea Grant

— Andrea Grant

Use the mirror below to write a prayer to God that reflects your feelings about your story. **Don't forget to EXPRESS YOUR FEELINGS LOUDLY!!!**

Andrea Grant

PRAYER
Changes Things !!!

Talk! It Helps to Get Your Feelings Out!

HAVE YOU THOUGHT ABOUT GETTING COUNSELING?

My Story:

My brother and I went to the child guidance center for years. There were things I couldn't discuss with my mom. I found it was much easier talking to my therapist about these things.

If things don't get better for you after this workbook, I want you to promise yourself that you will find someone to talk to who will help you with expressing your feelings.

Sign and date below to acknowledge your **official** commitment to getting the help that you need. *Don't move forward without considering how important this is!*

What Are My Thoughts Regarding Counseling?

Appreciate Your Second Chance at Life

> "It could've been *worse*. You could've been *dead*."
> — Lyfe Jennings

What If You Didn't Make It?

Some of us looked death right in the eye!!! We were just that close ... but we didn't die for a reason.

Find Your Reason for Being Here!

Everybody on earth is here on a mission. Find your mission and complete it!

What Is My Reason for Being Alive?

What Is My Mission?

How Can I Complete My Mission?

Never Be Ashamed of Your Past, Your Present or Your Future

Your past prepares you for your present and your present helps you in the future.

MISTAKES WILL HAPPEN.

With perseverance, we focus on getting through.

I find that a lot of survivors are so ashamed of what happened to them that they carry past feelings of guilt, defeat, and embarrassment into their present life. **It's time to change that!!!**

Let's Get EXCITED About the Future!!!

Complete the following prompts:

I will not bring...

1.
2.
3.
4.
5.
6.
7.
8.
9.
10.

...into my future.

I Will DELETE ALL the Following...

Things That Hinder My Future:
1.
2.
3.
4.
5.
6.
7.
8.
9.
10.
11.
12.
13.
14.
15.
16.
17.
18.
19.
20.

I Will DO the Following Because ...

My Present and Future HAPPINESS Depends On:
1.
2.
3.
4.
5.
6.
7.
8.
9.
10.
11.
12.
13.
14.
15.
16.
17.
18.
19.
20.

I Will Not Be Ashamed of the Things I Did in My Past!!!

Things I Once Was Ashamed of in My Past:

1.
2.
3.
4.
5.
6.
7.
8.
9.
10.
11.
12.
13.
14.
15.
16.
17.
18.
19.
20.

Past experiences—both good AND bad—teach us things!

Find the value in your past experiences!

Use the mirror below to share what you learned from the past.

After Reviewing My Past, I Later Learned:

Create a New Normal for Yourself

Changing habits simply means changing things that you have labeled as "normal." We sometimes sink into routines that are not good for us. The repetition of the routines makes them normal. A good example of this is how we cover our scars...

When someone asks us about our scars or our story, we say that we are okay knowing that we actually are not okay, but we develop this routine as a "normal" reaction.

WHY DO THAT TO YOURSELF?

Find a NEW normal that benefits growth, good health and boosts your confidence. Make it normal to wear shorts in the summer or a dress to a dinner date.

If we wear a swimsuit to the pool, it's normal to use a simple cover up, yet it is *not* normal to sit on the side with jeans and a sweater on!!!

It's time to break the spirit of fear and low self-esteem!!!

I Can Create A NEW Normal By...

It's Time to BREAK the Spirit of Fear and Low Self-Esteem!!!

— Andrea Grant

Ease into Loving Life and YOURSELF All Over Again

Why Am I Angry About My Image?

Why Am I Bitter About My Image?

Why Am I Depressed About My Image?

What Have I Always Loved About ME?

What Do I Currently Love About ME?

What Can I Learn to Love About ME?

STEP 03. HOLD YOUR HEAD UP

At Shriners Hospital:

Every day, I would hear someone saying, "Hold your head up." They weren't saying it to keep me motivated, but very literally.

I needed to physically hold my head up!

I walked the hospital hallways with my head down a lot. Chin into my chest. The doctors finally told me, "Andrea, if you do not hold your head up, we have to give you a neck brace."

I told myself, "There's no way he's going to put a neck brace on my neck because my neck isn't broken!"

My mother encouraged doctors that the neck brace was the way to go and days later I was walking around with a neck brace. Over the years, that day has always stuck with me. I would catch myself looking down and quickly hold my head up!

LESSON

Hold Your Head Up!!!

Do not feel defeated! You've already won the battle!

Your scars are your victory stripes, so you've earned your WIN!!!

There IS a life beyond scars!

Look around you at different things that bring you JOY!

Beauty Beyond the Mirror: 12 Steps to Confidence

Hold Your Head UP!

Andrea Grant

You Have SURVIVED !!!

EXERCISE

What Brings You Joy?

Where Do I Find JOY?		
People	Places	Things

How Can I MAXIMIZE My Joy Using This List?

5 People Who Bring JOY to My Life:

5 Things I Like Doing:

5 Places I Want to Visit in My Lifetime:

5 Experiences I Want to Share:

STEP 04. "DON'T STARE! ASK ME MY STORY!"

It's a fact:

People Will Stare at You Because You Are DIFFERENT!

My Story:

I had to learn to be okay with the stares of others. Being honest with you, I use to have a 5-second rule. I would give people time to look and then I would wait for them to ask. Most of the people who stared wouldn't ask me anything. I would just burst out loud and say,

"I was in a house fire. These are my scars."

On the other hand, my family disliked when people would stare at me. They would be so rude to people and ask, **"What are you staring at?"**

I know many survivors can relate.

Embarrassed, I would mumble and say, "They are looking at my scars."

"Well, they shouldn't just sit and stare at you!"

Before Kendell and I returned to school, Shriners Hospital sent a video to our school. The school assembled all the students in the auditorium to watch it. The video was images and information on how we would look once we returned to school with our garments on. That helped a lot because once we were back at school, everyone welcomed us with open arms.

Our schoolmates weren't afraid of our new look.

Outside of school, children would see us and immediately take off running. Over the years, there were many times when we would be in the toy aisle in a store and a child would be on the same aisle. One look at me and they would act like they had seen Freddy Krueger! That would make me feel so ugly! My entire mood would change. I hated going to the grocery store, big shopping centers, the mall and most of all... theme parks.

Once I started Beyond Scars, I created a shirt that reads,

"DON'T STARE! ASK ME MY STORY!"

I started wearing that shirt to the places I was once hesitant to visit. After the shirt was made, going to these places became therapy for me because people actually say, "Well young lady, I would like to know your story."

NOW! Pretend it's you! If someone made this statement, what would YOU say?

"Well, I would like to know your story."

Enter your response here:

And, yes! I know we've mentioned your story already, but practice makes perfect! You have to get comfortable with being uncomfortable so you can be **empowered** by telling your story and also **empower others along the way**!!!

"You will care less about what other people think of you when you realize who you are"

— Andrea Grant

After skin grafts, most burns have a diamond shape.

Growing up, I would hear mean things like:

"Fish Skin!"

"Waffle Shaped Skin."

"Burnt Up Skin!"

...and most recently, I've been called:

"A Burnt-Up French Fry!"

The TRUTH of my reality is this:

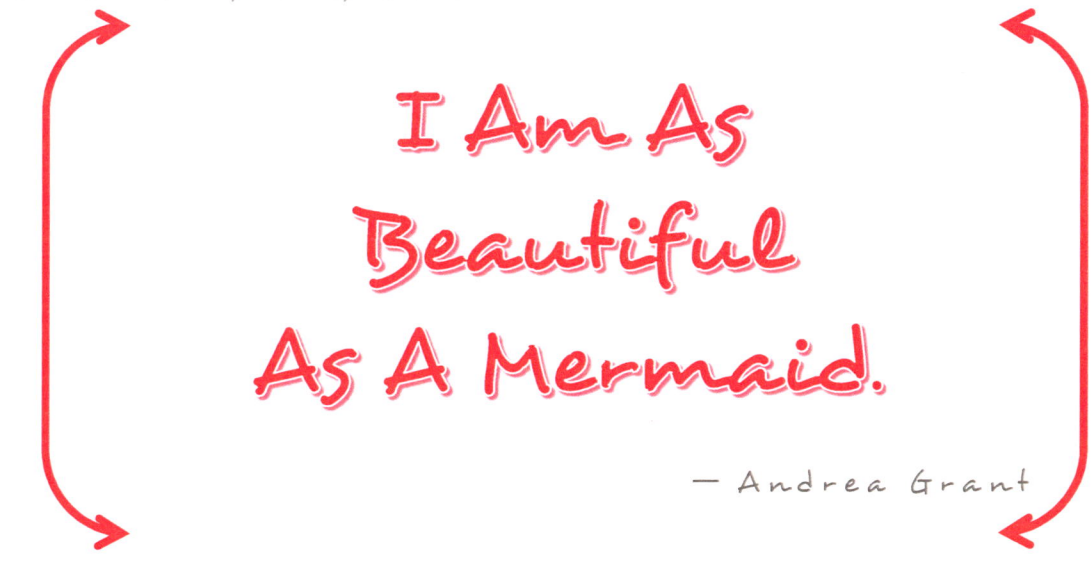

I Am As Beautiful As A Mermaid.

— Andrea Grant

LESSON

You may not feel comfortable with showing your scars just yet. Eventually, you will understand that your scars are like tattoos. They have meaning and stories behind them, and people *want* to know your story!

EXERCISE

Write Confidence Quotes

First, I want you to relax. Look at your scars. Begin to love on them. Love on yourself. Using the example quotes that I have provided, come up with some confidence quotes of your own.

> I Survived War Against the Fire.
> My Scars Are My Medals.
> # I Won!
> — Andrea Grant

> I Won't Be Ashamed of
> The Way I Look
> My Scars Are My Testimony!
> — Andrea Grant

> # DON'T STARE!
> ## Ask Me My Story!
> — Andrea Grant

Now, it's your turn! Write/Draw some BIG confidence quotes of your own here:

— (Write Your Name Here)

— (Write Your Name Here)

— (Write Your Name Here)

How Do I Feel When People Stare?

What Are the Bad Names I've Been Called?

What Are the Good Names I've Been Called?

What Good Names Do I Call Myself?

T-Shirt

If you could design a shirt to help others understand, what would it say??? Draw it here:

[ ]

Find a local t-shirt printing company that can create this shirt for you. Wear it to your most uncomfortable place to be...

What Were the Results???

_____
_____
_____
_____

How Did Designing the Tee Make Me Feel?

How Did Wearing the Tee Make Me Feel?

How Did the Process Help My Confidence?

What Did I Learn Through That Activity?

STEP 05. LOOK THE PART

Dress Confidently!

My Story:

While my hair was growing back, my mother would accessorize my hair with cute little headbands for my baby 'fro. I had every color to match all my outfits.

She made sure I always felt beautiful.

Eventually, I forgot about the scars on my legs. I wore skirts and shorts just like all the other kids because I was confident!

Confidence is Apparent in the Way You Carry Yourself.

The way I carry myself makes people want to know who I am... beyond my scars.

LESSON

During your recovery process and in the years to come, you may find items that you feel beautiful in. Shopping is a stress reliever for some people, but I know having on the right jeans or dress is a confidence booster for all women!

> "All White Everything"
> — Young Jeezy

When you are out,

Be "YOU" tiful!

The color white has been my signature color for years.

I try to shy away from prints because they clash with my scars in my opinion.

Find what color you feel most beautiful in and wear it. Often!

What color will you wear more of? Write it here:

"Loving yourself is the essence of true beauty and confidence! Makeup just enhances what is already there".

— -Kimberley Jacques, MUA

Be yourself! Know that accessories and clothing are material things that add flavor to your scars!

Accessories That Add Flavor to My Scars

Tops That Add Flavor to My Scars

Bottoms That Add Flavor to My Scars

Colors That Add Flavor to My Scars

"I'm gonna take a deep breath.
I'm gonna hold my head up.
I'm gonna put my shoulders back and look you straight in the eye.
Gonna flirt with somebody when they walk by..."

— Fantasia Barrino

EXERCISE

Fake It 'til You Make It!

If you know that you *look* like a confident person, eventually you'll start to *feel* like one too!

Be Approachable!

Hold your head up and put your shoulders back when you walk.

Try these tips:

1. **Smile Often**
   Smile because a smile changes your attitude, raises your confidence, and makes you more attractive. Making yourself smile (regardless of how you feel) actually changes the way you feel. You will automatically feel better.

2. **Chin Up!!**
   While speaking, holding your head down is not a mark of confidence. It carries the message, "I am not very comfortable or confident in who I am."

3. **Have Approachable Body Language**
   Adopt confident body language. You will feel more confident *and* people will want to approach you and engage. This is especially true if you're in the dating field, so be sure that you are sending the right signals or signals will get crossed! ☺

4. **Introduce Yourself First**
   This has always worked for me,
   Hi, I'm (Write Your Name Here)!
   I'm a (Write Who You Are OR Your Title).

Here are some other confidence tips:

5. **When You Walk into A Room, OWN IT!**
6. **Make Eye Contact When You Speak**

How Have These Tips Helped Me??

"Your perfect imperfection is what makes you The Most Beautiful Girl in the world!"

— Auntie Mateshia

"...most of all I'm thankful for lovin' who I really am! I'm beautiful! Yes, I'm beautiful and I'm here!"

— Fantasia Barrino

STEP 06. BOUNCE BACK!

In my 15 years of being a burn survivor I have noticed that when you are burnt as an adult, you are more likely to give up before the scars thoroughly heal.

This is a result of knowing what life was like prior to your accident. You know who you were before. You know pain and you know what life was like years and years before the fire.

As children, we find it easier to "bounce back." We may experience childhood depression, yet it's easier to assure a child that things are going to be okay than it is to encourage an adult. The adult might feel that those are just empty words we say to make it through...

My Story:

> While being in the hospital, I remember when we would go to the play room. Kids who had no arms were laughing and kicking a ball. Even with no arms, they found great joy in tossing the ball around with their feet. It was clear that these children were eager to find other ways to enjoy life. They were open to options...
>
> I would get bribed into going to the tub room. I was cool with that...
>
> If you knew you would get a lollipop, it didn't matter how much pain you had to endure, you knew there was a reward at the end. That reward—no matter how small—made all the pain worth it.

That's what happens with children. Adults—on the other hand—are not like the kids. Adults do not have these child-like attachments to happiness. Therefore, their road to recovery is much harder.

- *Depression knows the mind because it has been there before.*

- *Doubt knows the mind because it has been there before.*

- *Pain knows the mind because it has been there before.*

Depression. Doubt. Pain.

When we experience trauma as adults, these things hit you with *all* they have! They become harder to get rid of once they set in...

Addiction is more likely to happen in teens and adults because they can find several ways to escape and ultimately cope.

I want you to know that age matters in the road to recovery!!!

Do not let death win! Fight harder! Find other avenues of survival that have worked in the years prior to having burns.

The adult mind knows love. It knows family. It knows faith, and most of all, it knows how to endure.

LIFE IS NOT OVER!!!

Staying in bed, just because you can, only makes you weaker—both mentally and physically.

- *If you think sick, you will be the sickest.*
- *If you think sad, you will be the saddest.*

There is someone somewhere who needs to hear your story and how you survived. Through leaning on the positive, you can increase your chance of survival.

Remember this: You are STILL breathing, so you have already beat the fire!

Write Two Related Quotes of Your Own. Share Your Bounce Back Mottos:

STEP 07. FLASHBACKS

Flashback –

"a sudden and disturbing vivid memory of an event in the past, typically as the result of psychological trauma..." ("flashback - Google Search", 2016)

Don't you hate when that happens?

My Story:

Still... 15 years later, I can sit in a room and if it's too quiet, I'll suddenly look around and the moment the house exploded replays in my head! I always think to myself, "What if this room just blows up???" Sometimes, a certain smell, place or thing can trigger a flashback. Pumping gas was once hard for me! My mind automatically told me the car was going to explode.

I can also share with you...

After one of my flashbacks, I developed anxiety attacks. This particular flashback occurred while I was riding in the car years back with my family. I heard a big BOOM! Maybe it was from a nearby navy base or a construction site—I don't know. For me, it meant DANGER!!! I immediately panicked! I reached for the car door. I tried to escape!!! I yelled to my mother that the car was about to blow up! I could smell fire although she reminded me that fire was not near, but for me... it was!

My eyes stretched! My heart pounded! I was scared and I was TERRIFIED. My mother assured me that the car was not going to explode...

Breathe, Andrea...

Breathe.

Look around you. Look!

Everything is ok!

Breathe.

LESSON

In the time of a flashback, remind yourself, "This is not real! This has happened *before*, but it is NOT happening *now*."

1. **Look at Your Surroundings.**
   Remind yourself of where you are, who is around you and what you see in that moment.

2. **BREATHE! Inhale and Exhale**
   When we are afraid, we breathe too quickly and shallowly. Our body begins to panic because we're getting rid of too much carbon dioxide. This causes dizziness, shakiness, and more panic. Breathing slowly and deeply will stop the panic.

3. **Repeat: I Have Survived! I Already Survived! I Have Won This Battle!**
   Focus on anything that will help you remember who you are now, particularly in regards the strength that you have.

EXERCISE

Write It Down.

When you feel ready, write down all you can remember about the flashback and how you got through it.

Write down anything you can think of that triggered the flashback. This will help you to remember information for your healing and to remind you that you did get through it before and that you can—and you will—get through it again.

To anticipate your flashbacks and responses, jot down your triggers here:

My Triggers	

STEP 08. ACHIEVING GOALS

A great confidence booster is completing a goal you've set for yourself.

Over the years, I've set all my goals as short-term goals because I feel that when you set long term goals, you put in your mind you have TIME to get it done. As a result, you become lazy. Not achieving a goal can block your true confidence from coming forth. Start with small projects you've been wanting to complete.

LESSON

Trying to take on a huge project or task can be overwhelming and intimidating for anyone! Instead, try breaking off small chunks. Do a little at a time. Small, little achievements make you feel good and they add up! Before you know it, you will have completed so many tasks!!!

Learn to work like this all the time, and you'll be a self-confidence maniac! I used this method even with writing this workbook and my book! I must say...

It is REALLY Working!!!

Your turn! What's on your to-do list that has been sitting there for a while?

To Do List:
1.
2.
3.
4.
5.
6.
7.
8.
9.
10.

What Are My Short-Term Goals:

1.
2.
3.
4.
5.
6.
7.
8.
9.
10.
11.
12.
13.
14.
15.
16.
17.
18.
19.
20.

What Are My Long-Term Goals:

1.
2.
3.
4.
5.
6.
7.
8.
9.
10.
11.
12.
13.
14.
15.
16.
17.
18.
19.
20.

STEP 09. ARE YOU A VICTIM OR SURVIVOR?

Victim —
a person "killed" as a result of a crime, accident, or other event... ("victim - Google Search", 2016)

Survivor —
a person who survives, especially a person remaining alive after an event in which others have died. ("survivor - Google Search", 2016)

Some people use the term "victim" over "survivor." I personally am a big fan of using "survivor!" I encourage others to use this as well.

The words "survivor" and "victim" have very different connotations *[a feeling that a word invokes in addition to its primary meaning ("connotation - Google Search", 2016)]*.

Being a "victim" implies helplessness and pity.

When people label me as a burn victim, I see it as an insult to the fact that I SURVIVED! So many survivors write me and say, "Hi! I'm a burn victim," and I immediately want to help them understand, "NO! You are NOT a victim! You are a burn SURVIVOR!"

What I really love about the term "survivor" is that it implies that you overcame—that you've WON! You were able to take control, and even though your inner or physical scars may still be healing, you did not die in the battle!

Survivors have scars.
Victims have graves.
— Unknown

My Story:

On my road to recovery, I myself did not know my identity. I was a victim because I thought as a victim. I felt like I had died inside and the person I once was no longer existed and was physically gone. I had to accept the new me— Andrea, SURVIVOR, with scars over 80 percent of her body.

LESSON

Choose your words carefully and POWERFULLY! Empowering yourself in the aftermath of a traumatic and life-changing experience is definitely not easy. However, making this vocabulary switch can impact the healing process in a positive way for you.

EXERCISE

Now, let's practice!

Say these affirmations out loud:

- I Am a Survivor!
- I Did Not Die!
- I Am No Longer a Victim!
- I Will Not Label Myself as A Victim!
- I Am More Than Conquer!
- I Survived!

Create a few Affirmations of Your Own:

- _____
- _____
- _____
- _____
- _____

"I survived because the fire inside me burned brighter than the fire around me."

— Joshua Graham

What Made Me Feel Like a Victim?

What Makes Me Feel Like a Survivor Now?

Step 10. Let Go

Before we can be confident in who we are now, we must let go of grudges, guilt, and hurt that we feel.

We must forgive but never forget these lessons along the road to recovery. To find happiness, we must let go of what attached itself and snatched our happiness away from us. We must vow to NEVER let the power of pain put us in a shell again!

Lesson

Survivors have so many different stories.

You may have lost a loved one in the fire...

...Maybe you didn't change the smoke detector...

...You may be like my brother and me when we didn't turn around and walk back out of the door...

...Perhaps, you couldn't save everyone...

Some survivors even wish they died in the fire. That might be your story too. You may hold resentment for any number of reasons!

This list goes on. Whatever it is that you personally need to let go of...

START NOW!

"Throughout the course of my life, I will forgive myself."

— Ann Patchett

Why is it Important for Me to Let Go?

EXERCISE

For the next 5 days, find a painful attachment that you are holding onto and LET GO!

Day 1: TODAY I'm Letting Go Of….

Day 2: TODAY I'm Letting Go Of....

Day 3: TODAY I'm Letting Go Of....

Day 4: TODAY I'm Letting Go Of....

Day 5: TODAY I'm Letting Go Of....

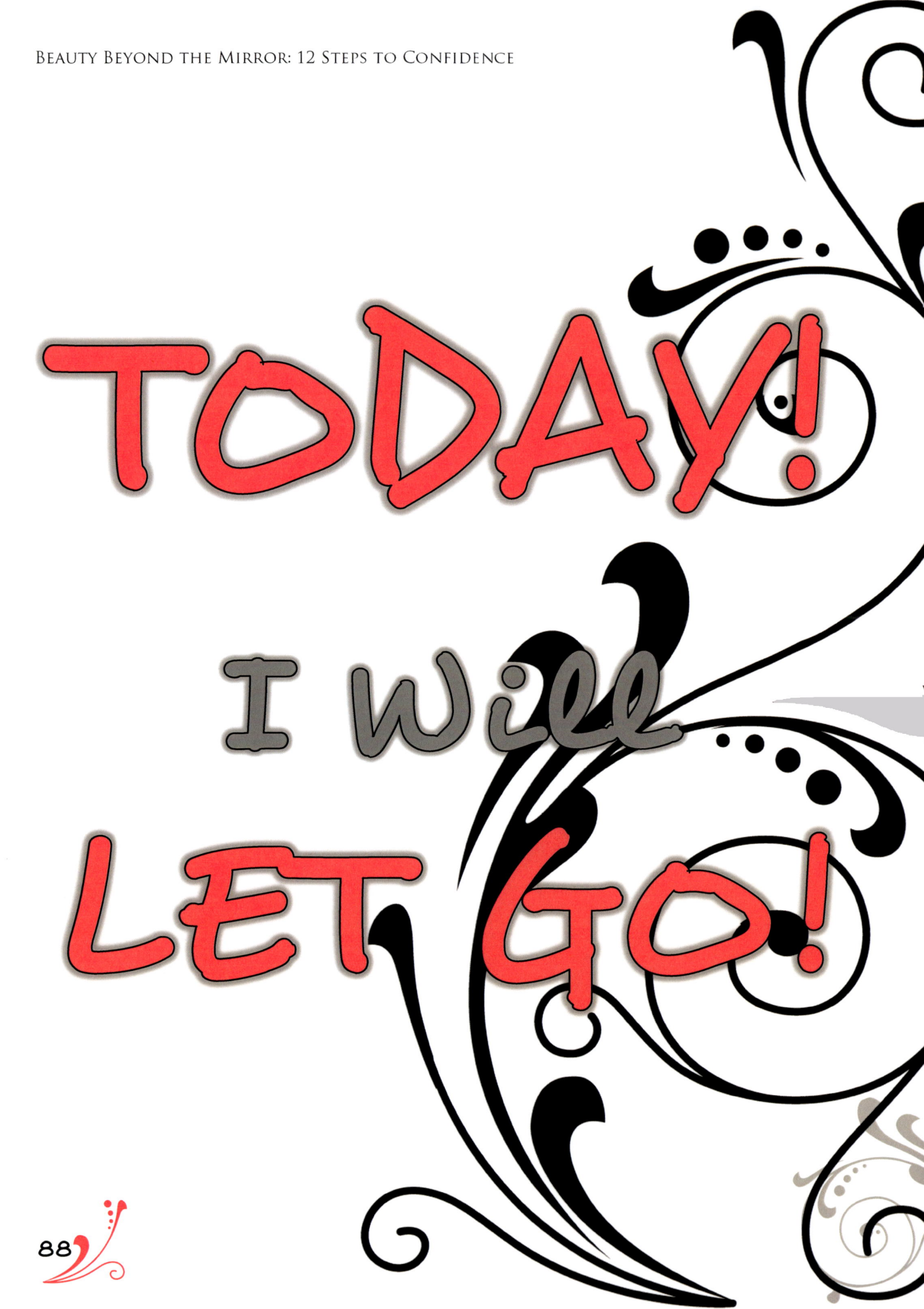

STEP 11. BE A LADDER

As I encourage you, you must encourage someone else.

Somewhere there is another survivor introducing themselves as a victim! We must stick together and share the lessons we have learned.

Every day, over 3,000 people are burned around the world. The road to recovery is just like a race. Now that I have passed the baton to you, you must pass the baton to someone else.

LESSON

God is using you as an instrument to inspire someone else. He brought you through so that you will be able to reach through the fire and pull someone else OUT!!!

I can't physically touch everyone but I pray this book finds itself in the hands of every burn survivor who is still living life in the ashes.

> *"He wants your ashes to give you beauty."*
>
> — Isaiah 61:3

EXERCISE

- *Volunteer*
- *Join a local support group or start one of your own!*

Volunteer -

Many camps, hospitals and organizations have volunteer opportunities.

Search online for outreach programs that fit your likes and your location!

Find 3 volunteer groups that you LOVE and participate in them regularly!

1.
2.
3.

Support Groups

If you can't find a local support group in your area, you can always start a support group for survivors in your city. That's how I started Beyond Scars.

Do it and continue it even if just a few people join you.

My Story:

My first support group meeting was held in a friend's boutique. It was me and two other burn survivors.

I purchased pens and notebooks for the survivors and we wrote down what we wanted to gain by joining the support group.

The next meeting was held at a local library conference room. There were over ten survivors and their family members.

The Beyond Scars support group continues to grow. Each meeting, we have more survivors...

Not all have burns.

During my meetings, I have words printed out on big cards.

The words include:

- Addiction
- Depression
- Faith
- Motivation
- Perseverance
- Prayer
- Self-Esteem
- Stares

We pass these cards around at every meeting.

Each person picks a card and speaks on how the term affects them.

Use these tips and tools for the support group that you join OR create!

STEP 12.   YOU ARE A SURVIVOR!!!

You Made It!

You have arrived at the final step: an assessment of your confidence!!!

Before we begin, let's start by reviewing how you FIRST felt after the trauma.

How Did It Feel to Be a VICTIM?

NOW, use the below assessment to rate your NEW confidence.

If you find areas where you need more work, revisit the sections of the book until you get to a GREAT place of confidence and realize that you ARE a **SURVIVOR**!

1. Who was most influential in assisting you with understanding that "It Happened?"
   _____ *Send a small token of appreciation to this person.*

2. Was the feedback that you received from family and friends helpful? YES NO

3. Are you more comfortable telling your story to others? YES NO

4. Have you arrived at the point of ACCEPTANCE for your experience? YES NO

5. How has your view of yourself changed since completing these steps to confidence?
   _____
   _____
   _____
   _____
   _____

6. How has your view of your life changed since completing these steps to confidence?
   _____
   _____
   _____
   _____
   _____

7. How has your mindset changed since completing these steps to confidence?
   _____
   _____
   _____
   _____
   _____

8. Where did you find your JOY?   People   Places   Things   Experiences

9. Are you more comfortable with the stares of others now?   YES   NO

   I know this is a step we endure forever because our scars are new to new people.

10. How has your reaction to the stares changed? _____
    _____
    _____
    _____
    _____
    _____

11. What have you upgraded about your look since starting the workbook? _____
    _____
    _____
    _____
    _____
    _____

12. At your age, have you found ways to bounce back?   YES   NO

13. Do you realize life is not over and that you still have purpose?   YES   NO

14. Have you learned the best ways for you to get through a flashback?   YES   NO

15. How do you introduce yourself now? **As a VICTIM**   *or*   **As a SURVIVOR**

16. Are you satisfied with the goals you have been able to achieve?   YES   NO

17. Have you found forgiveness?   YES   NO

   STOP NOW and Repeat This Out Loud:

   ## I am no longer holding grudges or guilt. I have let go and found forgiveness.

18. Have you been a ladder and encouraged another survivor?   YES   NO

19. Have you passed the baton by sharing what you learned in this book?   YES   NO

20. Finally... **ARE YOU CONFIDENT?** Have these steps truly helped you?   YES   NO

How Does It FEEL to Be a SURVIVOR?

CLOSING LETTER

Dear Survivor,

YOU DID IT!!!

You were built to last my friend and I am very proud of you! Pat yourself on the back because you have completed your 12 Steps to Confidence and you did not give up!

I am sure you have noticed the people around you go through less than you and they can't handle normal life situations. They are breaking and ready to give up, but you didn't!

It takes a strong mind to survive a traumatic situation and seek help or ways to heal.

God already knew our path. Our journey in life was pre-written and He knew we would be strong enough to endure the pain...

"You were picked out to be picked on."
— Katana Campbell

You are a SURVIVOR and the moment you chose to continue to live, you showed PROOF that YOU were built to last!

I am excited about your future!

Sincerely,
Andrea Grant

Thank You for Letting Me Help You Find…

References

connotation - Google Search. (2016). *Google.com*. Retrieved 1 January 2017, from https://www.google.com/search?q=connotation

flashback - Google Search. (2016). *Google.com*. Retrieved 1 January 2017, from https://www.google.com/search?q=flashback

survivor definition - Google Search. (2016). *Google.com*. Retrieved 1 January 2017, from https://www.google.com/search?q=survivor+definition

victim - Google Search. (2016). *Google.com*. Retrieved 1 January 2017, from https://www.google.com/search?q=victim

www.ingramcontent.com/pod-product-compliance
Lightning Source LLC
Chambersburg PA
CBRC090904080526
44588CB00006B/80